Capstone Short Biographies

African-American Inventors III

Patricia Bath, Philip Emeagwali, Henry
Sampson, Valerie Thomas, Peter Tolliver

by Susan K. Henderson

Content Consultant:
Robert L. Mason, Ph.D.
Phenomenologist
Formerly with Chicago Public Schools

CAPSTONE BOOKS
an imprint of Capstone Press
Mankato, Minnesota

C A P S T O N E   P R E S S
818 North Willow Street • Mankato, MN 56001
http://www.capstone-press.com

Library of Congress Cataloging-in-Publication Data
Amram, Fred M.B.
    African-American inventors / Fred M.B. Amram
    p. cm.
    Includes bibliographical references and index.
    Summary: Brief biographical profiles of five African-American
inventors.
    ISBN 1-56065-361-2
        1. Afro-American inventors--Biography--Juvenile literature.
[1. Inventors. 2. Afro-Americans--Biography.] I. Title.
T39.A55 1996
609.2'273--dc20

                                                95-47863
                                                CIP
                                                AC r96

Henderson, Susan K. *African-American Inventors III.* ISBN 1-56065-698-0

Editorial credits:
Editor, Rebecca Glaser; cover design and illustrations, James Franklin;
    photo research, Michelle L. Norstad

Photo credits:
Archive Photos, 4
Patricia Bath, cover, 8, 10
Philip Emeagwali, 14, 16, 18, 21
International Stock/John Zoiner, 40
Jeff Fearing, 13
NASA, 25
Cindy Roalson, 39
Henry T. Sampson, 22
Valerie Thomas, 28, 30
Peter Tolliver, 34
U.S. Patent Office, 6, 26, 33, 37, 44

Table of Contents

Chapter 1

What Inventors Do

George Washington Carver was a famous African-American inventor. He invented more than 100 uses for peanuts. Some of the uses included ink, medicine, and glue.

Inventors are people who create new things or improve old ones. They try to solve problems and think of better ways to do things. Their inventions can make life easier, safer, and more fun.

Some inventors study engineering in college. Engineering is using the rules of math and science to build and create things. Their inventions might help doctors keep people healthy. Or they might make space flight safer.

Inventors make some inventions at home. Everyday activities inspire them. Some of these inventions make chores easier.

George Washington Carver invented more than 100 uses for peanuts.

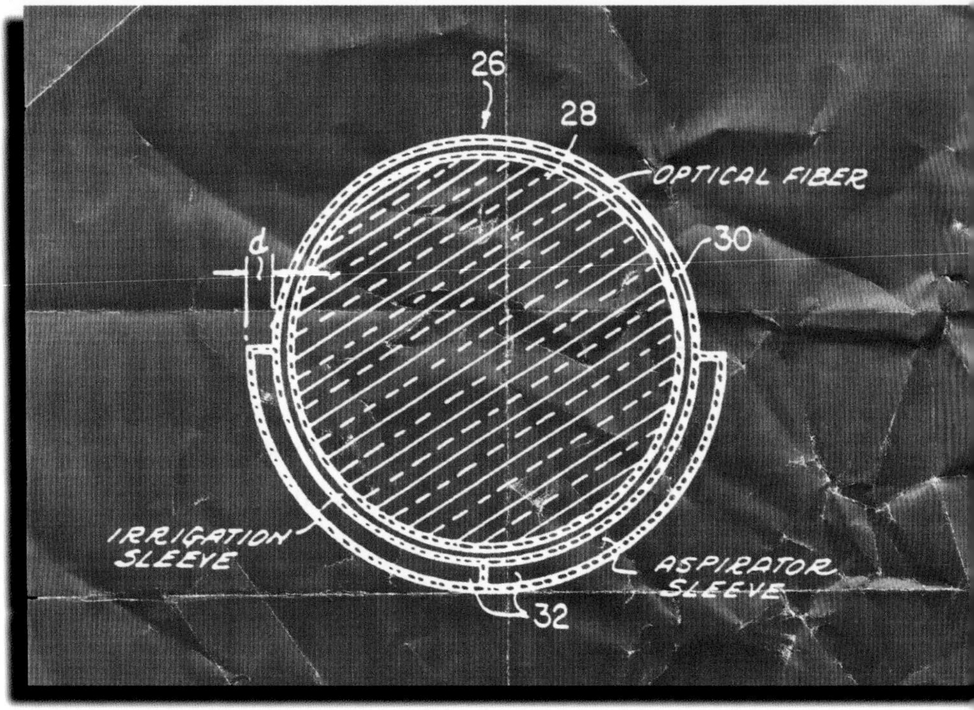
26
28
OPTICAL FIBER
30
d
IRRIGATION SLEEVE
ASPIRATOR SLEEVE
32

Inventors submit drawings along with patent applications.

Many inventions are objects. But a process or a plan can also be an invention. A process is a way of doing things.

Patent Protection

Inventors can apply for patents to protect their inventions. A patent is an official paper. It gives inventors the right to make and sell their inventions. A patent prevents others from making or selling the same invention for 17 years. The United States Patent and Trademark Office (USPTO) issues patents.

Inventors must do patent searches before they can receive a patent. A patent search is checking for patents on similar products or processes. Inventors apply for patents if no one else has patents on the same inventions. Inventors submit patent drawings along with the legal forms to apply for a patent.

Sometimes inventors hire patent attorneys. A patent attorney is a person trained in patent laws. Patent attorneys help inventors apply for patents. They may do patent searches for inventors. Patent attorneys make sure inventors fill out legal forms correctly.

Patent examiners at the USPTO must approve patents. Examiners check to see if the inventions are new and useful before they approve patents. New means that the invention must be different from other inventions. In patent law, useful means that the invention must work for its intended purpose.

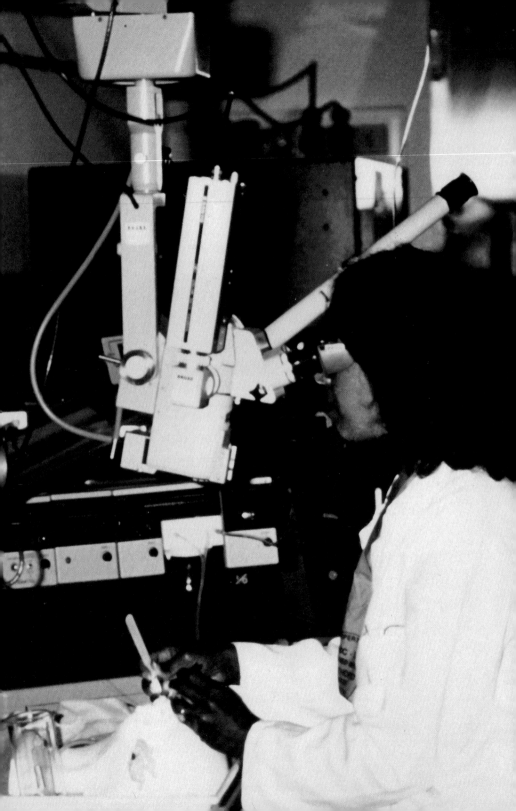

Chapter 2

Patricia Bath

1942–

Patricia Bath was born November 4, 1942, in New York City. She grew up in Harlem, New York. Her high school chemistry teacher encouraged her to apply for a National Science Foundation Scholarship. Bath won the scholarship. She began working with a research team at Yeshiva University and Harlem Hospital. Research means finding out about something by reading and doing experiments.

Bath became interested in medicine as a result of her work at Yeshiva University and Harlem Hospital. She graduated from Hunter College in New York in 1964. Then she went

Patricia Bath invented the laserphaco probe.

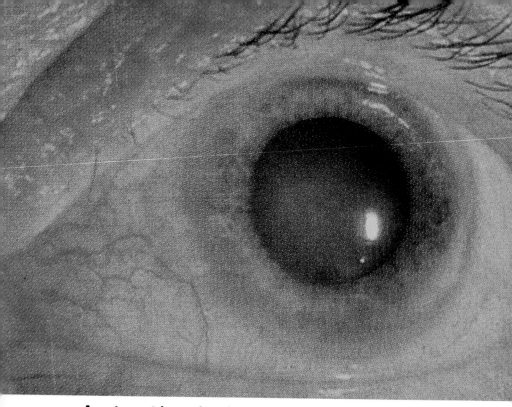

A cataract is a cloudy spot on a person's eye.

to medical school at Howard University in Washington, D.C.

After medical school, Bath taught as a professor at the University of California at Los Angeles School of Medicine. She researched laser systems in Berlin, Germany. In 1986, Bath invented the laserphaco probe. This device removes cataracts from people's eyes.

Cataracts

A cataract is a cloudy spot that can form on the lens of a person's eye. The lens of the human eye is normally clear. It helps the eye focus on objects. Cataracts can make a person partially or completely blind. A person can see clearly again after a doctor removes a cataract.

Doctors use ultrasound waves to break up cataracts. Ultrasound waves create vibrations that move back and forth in the air. These vibrations are too high for humans to hear. This motion can remove cataracts. Sometimes using ultrasound to remove cataracts damages patients' eyes.

New Laser Technology

Bath's laserphaco probe is a laser instrument used to remove cataracts. A laser is a device that produces a narrow and powerful beam of light.

Bath can aim the laserphaco probe's beam exactly where she wants it. The laser breaks up the cataract. It does not hurt any other part of the eye. Bath believes using new laser technology to remove cataracts is safer than using ultrasound.

Inventing and Testing

Bath began thinking about laser surgery for removing cataracts in the early 1980s. Surgery is medical treatment that involves repairing hurt or diseased parts of the body. Bath studied lasers in Germany and in the United States.

In 1986, Dr. Bath performed her first cataract surgery with her laserphaco probe. She did not test it on living people. Bath used the eyes of dead people. These people had given permission before they died for scientists and doctors to use their eyes.

Bath received a U.S. patent for the laserphaco probe in 1988. She later received patents in Japan, Canada, and Europe. Bath was the first African-American female doctor to earn a patent for a medical invention.

The Food and Drug Administration (FDA) is testing Bath's laserphaco probe. The FDA is part of the U.S. government that tests products to make sure they are safe. The FDA tests food, new medicines, and medical methods. The FDA must make sure the laserphaco probe is safe before anyone in the United States can use it.

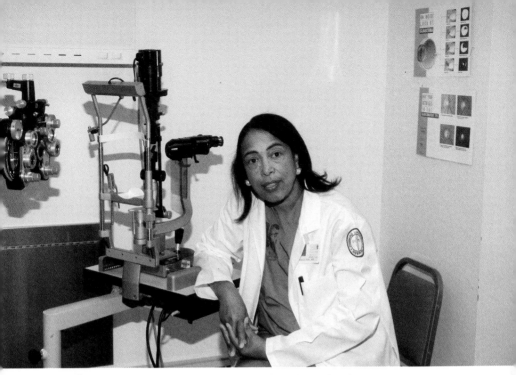
Bath was the first African-American female doctor to earn a patent for a medical invention.

Helping Others

Bath helped found the American Institute for Prevention of Blindness (AIPB) in 1978. The AIPB uses technology to teach people about eye health. It helps doctors around the world learn about new ways to take care of eyes.

This organization has donated eye-care equipment to needy clinics. It donated eye drops to eye clinics in Africa. The AIPB wants all people to have good eye care.

Chapter 3

Philip Emeagwali

1954–

Philip Emeagwali (eh-MAY-ah-gwah-lee) was born August 23, 1954, in Akure, Nigeria. Nigeria is in western Africa. He grew up in Nigeria. Emeagwali's friends in junior high called him Calculus. Calculus is an advanced form of math. They called him Calculus because he liked math so much.

People have to pay to go to school in Nigeria. Emeagwali had to quit school before he finished high school. It cost too much. He was one of nine children. His family could not afford to pay for his schooling.

Emeagwali taught himself by reading books and studying. He learned calculus, physics, chemistry, and the English language. Physics is

Philip Emeagwali studied math and engineering in college.

Emeagwali (far right) and his family lived in Nigeria.

the study of matter and energy. It includes the study of light, heat, sound, electricity, motion, and forces. Emeagwali took an exam from the University of London. He earned a General Certificate of Education (GCE) after he passed the exam in 1973. A person who has passed this test has similar skills to a high school graduate.

In 1974, Emeagwali moved to the United States to study. He studied math at Oregon State University. Emeagwali later studied engineering at George Washington University.

Emeagwali wanted to solve real problems using computers. He used his knowledge of math and engineering to program faster computers. Programming a computer means writing instructions to make it work in a certain way.

Supercomputers

A supercomputer is the fastest and most powerful computer available. The first supercomputers used large and complex computer processors. Complex means having many parts. A computer processor is the part of the computer that receives instructions and carries them out. Complex processors were expensive.

In 1989, Emeagwali programmed the Connection Machine to be the fastest computer in the world. The Connection Machine was a supercomputer made by Thinking Machines Corporation. Emeagwali programmed the Connection Machine to make 3.1 billion calculations per second. A calculation is a problem solved by using math. This speed was a new world record in 1989.

A New Kind of Supercomputer

The Connection Machine was a new kind of supercomputer. Emeagwali used parallel processing to program the Connection Machine. Parallel processing is using many computer processors at the same time to calculate one problem. The Connection Machine looked like a big, black box.

Emeagwali linked many computer processors over the NSFnet. The NSFnet was an early computer network similar to the Internet. Emeagwali programmed all the processors to calculate the same problem at the same time.

Uses for Parallel Processing

Parallel processing has many uses. Doctors may use it to look at three-dimensional pictures of the human body. Three-dimensional means appearing to have length, width, and height. These pictures can make operations easier. Scientists also use parallel processing to predict weather patterns.

Parallel processing also makes busy Internet sites work faster. Internet sites are places on the

Emeagwali used parallel processing to program the Connection Machine supercomputer.

Internet where people can find information. Busy Internet sites have several processors that work at the same time. Many more people can connect to the Internet site at the same time with parallel processing.

Helping Oil Companies

Emeagwali used parallel processing to help oil companies. He showed them how to recover more oil from under Earth's surface.

Engineers use advanced math and computers to predict where the most oil is. Predict means to guess what will happen in the future based on facts. Emeagwali helped oil company engineers make better predictions. He used different math calculations and parallel processing. His predictions were more accurate.

The record-breaking speed of Emeagwali's invention helped people understand the value of parallel computing. He showed that parallel computers could solve real problems.

Emeagwali has received many awards for parallel processing and computing. Emeagwali received the Gordon Bell Prize in 1989 for programming the Connection Machine. The Institute for Electrical and Electronics Engineers

Emeagwali used his math and computing skills to help oil companies.

awards the Gordon Bell Prize. The prize recognizes the use of supercomputers to solve important scientific and engineering problems.

The National Society of Black Engineers named Emeagwali Pioneer of the Year in 1996. They awarded him for his discoveries and inventions that led to the acceptance of parallel computing. Emeagwali's inventions have helped many people and businesses.

Chapter 4

Henry Sampson

1934–

Henry T. Sampson Jr. was born April 22, 1934, in Jackson, Mississippi. Sampson loved figuring out how to make small things work when he was young.

Sampson studied engineering in college. He earned a doctorate from the University of Illinois. A doctorate is the highest degree awarded by a university or college.

Sampson invented a new process for making rocket fuel. The new process made rocket fuel tanks less likely to explode. Sampson also invented a gamma electric cell that converts gamma radiation into electricity. Radiation is rays of energy given off by certain elements.

Henry Sampson invented a new way to make rocket fuel.

Rocket Fuel

Rockets are powered by solid propellant. Propellant is fuel used in rockets. Engineers make solid propellant from liquid propellant.

To make solid propellant, engineers used to pour liquid propellant into a tube. Each tube had a plastic liner. They baked the tubes filled with liquid propellant. The propellant became solid. Baking also bonded the propellant to the tube's plastic liner.

This method of making rocket fuel created one problem. The propellant sometimes shrank after it was baked. It separated from the plastic liner. This separation exposed too much of the propellant surface to air. The exposed propellant created too much pressure in rockets when it burned. The pressure sometimes made rockets explode.

Super Glue

Sampson invented a safe way to make propellant so that rockets would not explode. He read about a product called Eastman 910 Adhesive. Adhesive is a liquid or solid that makes objects stick together. This adhesive is now very

Rockets are powered by solid propellant.

common and is used for many household jobs. It is often called super glue.

Sampson sprayed the adhesive on the plastic liner inside the tube. Then he poured the liquid propellant into the tube. The new adhesive created a very strong bond between the propellant and the liner. Then he baked the propellant and tube.

With Sampson's method, the liner shrank with the propellant. The propellant was not

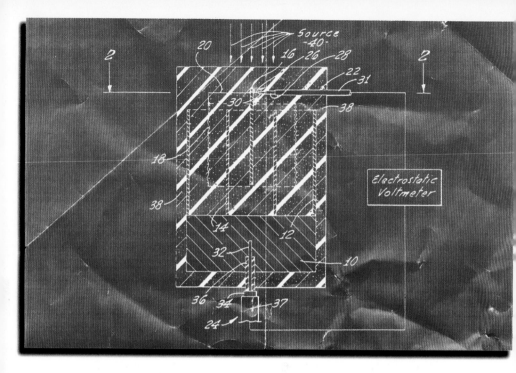

Sampson's gamma electric cell converts gamma rays into electricity.

exposed to air if it shrank. The space was between the liner and the tube. Sampson's method of making rocket propellant made rocket fuel tanks less likely to explode.

Sampson received a patent for his rocket propellant bonding process in 1961. Engineers used this process in missiles launched from submarines. A missile is an explosive that can fly long distances. Engineers also used the process in the space shuttle rockets. Sampson's process makes space flight safer because the rockets that power the space shuttle are less likely to explode.

Gamma Electric Cell

Sampson also invented a gamma electric cell. The gamma electric cell converts gamma rays into electricity. Gamma rays are a type of radiation. Sampson's gamma electric cell converts gamma rays directly into electricity. Sampson patented this device in 1971.

The U.S. government has used the gamma electric cell to detect radiation from nuclear weapons testing. Nuclear weapons are powerful bombs that leave behind harmful elements when they explode. The U.S. government tested nuclear weapons underground. The gamma electric cell converted the radiation left behind by the weapons into measureable electricity.

Sampson is an engineer for the Aerospace Corporation in California. He also collects rare African-American films. Sampson has written books on the importance of African-American contributions to the entertainment industry.

Chapter 5

Valerie Thomas

1943–

V alerie Thomas was born February 1, 1943, in Baltimore, Maryland. She was inventive as a child. She learned to use a sewing machine when she was seven. Thomas sewed clothes for her dolls, herself, and her mother.

Her father's hobby was electronics. He would often take apart televisions (TVs). Thomas saw the inside of a TV. She wondered how the parts inside made a picture on the screen.

She studied physics in college to learn how TVs and other things work. She later studied engineering, too.

Thomas worked for the National Aeronautics and Space Administration (NASA) for more

Valerie Thomas invented an illusion transmitter.

than 30 years. She created complex computer systems. The computer systems collected data from scientific satellites. A satellite is a spacecraft that orbits Earth.

The Light Bulb That Was Not There

Thomas once saw a science exhibit with light bulbs. She watched a man unscrew a light bulb from a lamp. But the light bulb was still there. She was surprised when she tried to touch the bulb. Her hand went through it. There was nothing there.

Thomas saw that the bulb was an illusion. An illusion is something that appears to exist but does not. A concave mirror was reflecting another light bulb to create the illusion. Concave means hollow and curved, like the inside of a bowl.

Real Images

A flat reflection appears inside a mirror. But the illusion that Thomas saw appeared in the air in front of the concave mirror. This type of illusion

There are concave mirrors inside the black dome. The ring hovering in the hole is a real image.

is called a real image. Real images appear to be three-dimensional.

Thomas wondered if she could figure out how to transmit real images over long distances. She thought businesses might use real images to present new products. Families might enjoy the illusion of having famous people appear in their living rooms. So Thomas invented an illusion transmitter.

Illusion Transmitter

Thomas' illusion transmitter works like a TV transmitter. A TV transmitter sends signals through the air. Thomas' illusion transmitter works the same way. But Thomas' transmitter also uses concave mirrors. The images bounce off a concave mirror before they are transmitted.

The image signals from the illusion transmitter are received on devices similar to TVs. These devices convert the signal into pictures, like a TV does. The devices also use concave mirrors to convert the signal into real images. The images appear in the air in front of the screen. They appear to be three-dimensional.

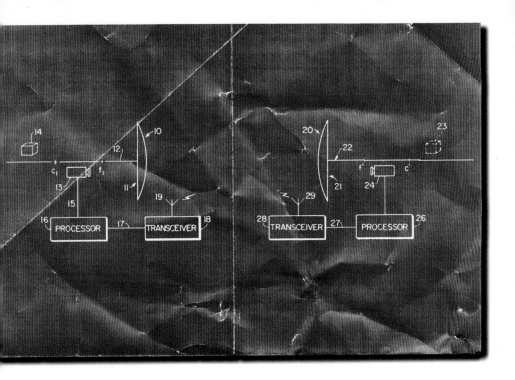

Thomas received a patent for the illusion transmitter in 1980.

Looking ahead

Thomas received a patent for the illusion transmitter in 1980. She has not yet made any money from her invention. The illusion transmitter is very expensive to make.

But other companies have used similar devices to create illusions. These companies use illusions to advertise their products.

Chapter 6

Peter Tolliver

1927–

Peter M. Tolliver was born in 1927 in
Nashville, Tennessee. He grew up in Tennessee.
He studied engineering and physics at Fisk
University. Physics is the study of matter and
energy. It includes the study of light, heat,
sound, electricity, and motion.

Tolliver taught physics after he received a
master's degree. A master's degree is the
second highest degree given by a university.
Tolliver later studied at the University of
Michigan. Tolliver was drafted while he was a
graduate student in Michigan. Drafted means
selected to serve in the U.S. armed forces.
Tolliver served in the Korean War (1950-1954).

Peter Tolliver received patents for nine inventions.

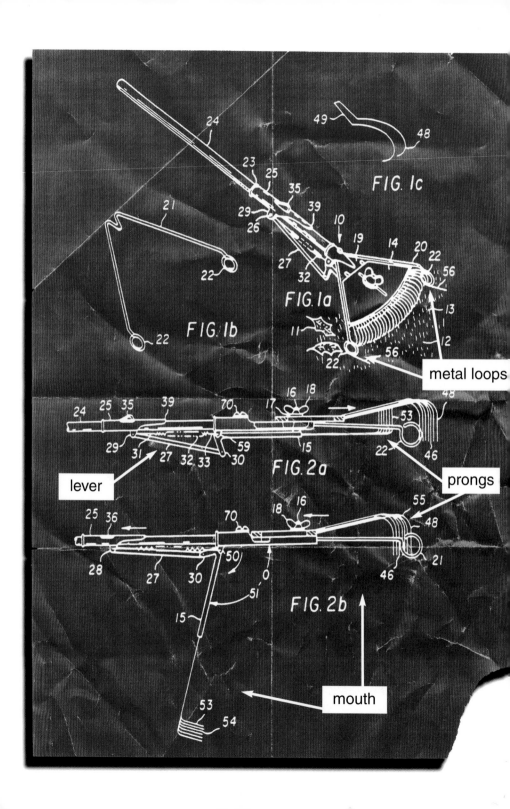

FIG. 1c

FIG. 1a

FIG. 1b

metal loops

lever

prongs

FIG. 2a

mouth

FIG. 2b

He worked as an engineer after he was released from the army.

Tolliver has always thought about ways of doing things better. He invents things that make life easier. Tolliver has received nine patents. Some of his inventions solved everyday problems. Five of his inventions are related to engineering and physics.

Making Raking Easier

Tolliver did not like bending over to pick up leaves after raking them. He thought there must be a better way to lift and remove leaves. So Tolliver invented a rake that let him rake and pick up leaves without bending over. The rake also moves through grass easily because it rides on metal loops.

Tolliver's rake has two sets of rake prongs connected to one handle. The two sets of prongs face each other. The prongs form a mouth that can open and close. A lever on the handle operates the mouth.

Tolliver's rake has a mouth that can open and close.

Someone using Tolliver's rake first rakes leaves into a pile. The person uses the lever to open the rake's mouth over the pile. Next, the person closes the rake mouth on the leaves and carries them off. The person uses the lever to open the rake mouth and drop the leaves in a container. The rake user does not have to bend down or touch the leaves.

Tolliver received a patent for his rake in 1994. Several companies have said they would sell the rake if he can get it manufactured. He is still trying to to find a company to manufacture it.

Fish Hooks

Tolliver has fished for trout for many years. He noticed that many trout escaped after biting his hooks. He wanted to catch more of those fish.

Tolliver invented an improved treble hook. A treble hook has three hooks joined together. The hook points on a regular treble hook all point forward. A fish must open its mouth wide to get caught on a regular treble hook.

The top hook is a regular treble hook. Tolliver's treble hook (bottom) makes catching fish easier.

Tolliver used differently shaped hooks. He bent his hooks at different angles. He made one hook longer than the others. His treble hook makes catching fish easier.

The fish do not have to open their mouths as wide to get caught. The fish are caught on the hook as soon they bite. Fewer fish are able to escape from Tolliver's treble hook.

Paper manufacturing companies use infrared moisture gauges.

Moisture Gauge

Tolliver also created scientific inventions. For example, he improved an industrial moisture gauge. Paper manufacturing companies use these gauges to measure the amount of moisture in paper. The amount of moisture affects the quality of the paper.

Companies use machines to produce paper in long rolls. Machines bathe the paper in water. Then machines squeeze out most of the water.

Moisture gauges work by shining infrared light through the paper sheet. Infrared light is light humans cannot see. This light also produces heat radiation. Moisture in the paper absorbs the radiation. The gauge measures how much light is absorbed. This tells workers the amount of moisture in the paper.

Tolliver invented a better way of shining infrared light through paper. Infrared light usually spreads out in a fan shape. But Tolliver used different shapes to make the light beams parallel. Tolliver's parallel light beams helped companies measure moisture in their paper products more accurately.

Tolliver has invented many other things. He invented a better staple remover and a long gun holster. His engineering background has helped him invent better tools.

Words to Know

adhesive (ad-HEE-siv)—a liquid or solid that makes objects stick together

cataract (KAT-uh-rakt)—a cloudy spot that can form on the lens of a person's eye

concave (kon-KAYV)—hollow and curved, like the inside of a bowl

gamma ray (GAM-muh RAY)—a type of radiation

illusion (i-LOO-zhuhn)—something that appears to exist but does not

infrared light (IN-fruh-red LITE)—light that produces heat; humans cannot see infrared light

Internet site (IN-tur-net SITE)—a place on the Internet where people can find information

laser (LAY-zur)—a device that produces a very narrow and powerful beam of light

parallel processing (PA-ruh-lel PROH-sess-ing)—using many computer processors at the same time to calculate one problem

programming (PROH-gram-ing)—writing instructions to make a computer work in a certain way

propellant (pruh-PEL-uhnt)—fuel used in rocket motors

radiation (ray-dee-AY-shuhn)—rays of energy given off by certain elements

supercomputer (SOO-pur-kuhm-pyoo-tur)—the fastest and most powerful computer available

three-dimensional (three-duh-MEN-shuhn-uhl)—having or appearing to have length, deepness, and height

ultrasound (UHL-truh-sound)—sound waves that are too high for humans to hear

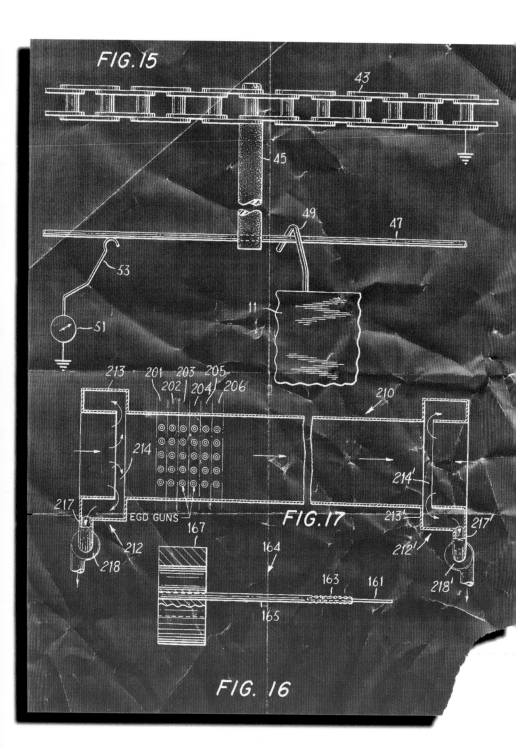

FIG.15

43

45

49

47

53

51

11

213 201 203 205
202 | 204 | 206

210

214

214'

217

EGD GUNS

213'

217'

212

218

167

164

212'

218'

163 161

FIG. 17

165

FIG. 16

To Learn More

Amram, Fred M. B. *African-American Inventors*. Mankato, Minn.: Capstone Press, 1996.

Hayden, Robert C. *9 African American Inventors*. Frederick, Md.: Twenty-First Century Books, Henry Holt and Co., Inc., 1992.

Henderson, Susan K. *African-American Inventors Volume II*. Mankato, Minn.: Capstone High-Low Books, 1998.

McKissack, Patricia and Fredrick. *African-American Inventors*. Brookfield, Conn.: Millbrook Press, 1994.

Patent drawings show the parts of inventions.

Useful Addresses

Black Inventions Museum, Inc.
P.O. Box 76122
Los Angeles, CA 90076

Canadian Intellectual Property Office
Industry Canada
Place du Portage, Phase I
50 Victoria Street
Hull, Quebec K1A 0C9
Canada

International Inventors Assistance League
345 West Cypress Street
Glendale, CA 91204

Inventors Clubs of America
P.O. Box 450261
Atlanta, GA 31145-0261

United States Patent and Trademark Office
2121 Crystal Drive
Arlington, VA 20231

Internet Sites

African-american (BLACK) Inventors Series
http://edcen.ehhs.cmich.edu/~rlandrum/
  index1.html

African Computer Wizard on the Net—
  Philip Emeagwali
http://emeagwali.com

3M Collaborative Invention Unit
http://mustang.coled.umn.edu/inventing/
  inventing.html

Three Dimensional Publishing's
  TDPNewsletter for Young Inventors
http://www.erols.com/tdpedu/yingl.htm

Young Inventors Network International Site
http://www.wirehub.nl/~invent/

Index